200 √

J

MAY YOU ENJOY THIS BOOK

The Public Library is free to all cardholders.
You can increase its usefulness to all by returning
books promptly, on or before the "Date Due"

If you derive pleasure and profit from the use of
your public library, please tell others about its
many services.

THE NASHUA PUBLIC LIBRARY
2 COURT STREET
NASHUA, NH 03060

D1265875

CHEECH MARIN

A Real-Life Reader Biography

Valerie Menard

Mitchell Lane Publishers, Inc.

P.O. Box 619
Bear, Delaware 19701

Copyright © 2002 by Mitchell Lane Publishers. All rights reserved. No part of this book may be reproduced without written permission from the publisher. Printed and bound in the United States of America.

First Printing

Real-Life Reader Biographies

Paula Abdul	Mary Joe Fernandez	Ricky Martin	Arnold Schwarzenegger
Christina Aguilera	Andres Galarraga	Mark McGwire	Selena
Marc Anthony	Sarah Michelle Gellar	Alyssa Milano	Maurice Sendak
Drew Barrymore	Jeff Gordon	Mandy Moore	Dr. Seuss
Brandy	Mia Hamm	Chuck Norris	Shakira
Garth Brooks	Melissa Joan Hart	Tommy Nuñez	Alicia Silverstone
Kobe Bryant	Jennifer Love Hewitt	Rosie O'Donnell	Jessica Simpson
Sandra Bullock	Faith Hill	Rafael Palmeiro	Sinbad
Mariah Carey	Hollywood Hogan	Gary Paulsen	Jimmy Smits
Cesar Chavez	Katie Holmes	Freddie Prinze, Jr.	Sammy Sosa
Christopher Paul Curtis	Enrique Iglesias	Julia Roberts	Britney Spears
Roald Dahl	Derek Jeter	Robert Rodriguez	Sheryl Swoopes
Oscar De La Hoya	Steve Jobs	J.K. Rowling	Shania Twain
Trent Dimas	Michelle Kwan	Keri Russell	Liv Tyler
Celine Dion	Bruce Lee	Winona Ryder	Robin Williams
Sheila E.	Jennifer Lopez	Cristina Saralegui	Vanessa Williams
Gloria Estefan	**Cheech Marin**		Tiger Woods

Library of Congress Cataloging-in-Publication Data
Menard, Valerie.
    Cheech Marin: a real-life reader biography / Valerie Menard.
        p. cm. — (A Real-life reader biography)
    Includes index.
    Filmography: p.
    ISBN 1-58415-070-X
        1. Marin, Cheech—Juvenile literature. 2. Motion picture actors and actresses—United States—Biography—Juvenile literature. 3. Hispanic American motion picture actors and actresses—United States—Biography—Juvenile literature. [1. Marin, Cheech. 2. Actors and actresses. 3. Mexican Americans—Biography.] I. Title. II. Series.
PN2287.M483 M46 2001
791.43'028'092—dc21
[B]   2001029088

ABOUT THE AUTHOR: Valerie Menard has been an editor for *Hispanic* magazine since the magazine moved to Austin, Texas, in July 1994. Before joining the magazine, she was a managing editor of a bilingual weekly, *La Prensa*. Valerie writes from a Latino perspective and as an advocate for Latino causes. She is the author of several biographies for children including *Oscar De La Hoya, Cristina Saralegui*, and *Salma Hayek* (Mitchell Lane) and the author of the newly published *Latinos: Traditional Celebrations, Modern Realities* (Marlowe).

PHOTO CREDITS: cover: Ethan Miller/Corbis; p. 4 Cheech Marin; p. 8 Globe Photos; pp. 12, 14 Kobal Collection; p. 17 AP; pp. 20, 28 Kobal Collection; p. 29 top & bottom Globe Photos.

ACKNOWLEDGMENTS: The following story has been thoroughly researched, and to the best of our knowledge, represents a true story. While every possible effort has been made to ensure accuracy, the publisher will not assume liability for damages caused by inaccuracies in the data, and makes no warranty on the accuracy of the information contained herein. This story has been written based on the author's personal interviews with Cheech Marin. It has been approved for print by him.

Table of Contents

Chapter 1
From *Chicharrón* to Comedian

It's difficult to describe the many faces of Cheech Marin. He has played an easy-living hippie, a *cholo* (homeboy), a misplaced Chicano, and a Mexican war hero. But in all the roles that he's taken in more than 25 years in Hollywood, he has always proudly played a Latino.

Cheech's real name is Richard Antonio Marin, and he was born in 1946 in East Los Angeles, California. He earned his nickname when he was very young. His uncle Urbano looked at him in the crib, saw a shriveled baby and remarked, "He looks like a *chicharrón*."

In all the roles he's taken in Hollywood, he has always proudly played a Latino.

That's an Hispanic snack made of deep-fried pork skins, and "cheech" is short for it.

Cheech discovered early on that he had a talent for music. At the age of five, he recorded and released his first song, "Amorcito Corazón." He learned to play the guitar when he was twelve, and during his school years he sang with a neighborhood rock band.

Cheech's parents were born in Los Angeles and are of Mexican descent. He is the third generation of his family to live in the United States. His father, Oscar, was a police officer for the Los Angeles Police Department (LAPD) for over 30 years. After he retired, he taught criminology (the study of crime) at Valley College in Los Angeles. Cheech says his father was very strict, and they butted heads a great deal when he was growing up. "Today, though, we get along very well," he reveals.

Cheech's mother, Elsa, stayed home with the kids. "She was always loving and nurturing," remembers Cheech.

Cheech and his family are from Los Angeles and are of Mexican descent.

The oldest of four children, he and his three sisters, Margie and Monica (twins) and Elena, grew up in an African-American neighborhood in downtown Los Angeles. When Cheech was ten, his family moved to a more mixed neighborhood in Granada Hills. The move from an almost all-African-American neighborhood to an all-white neighborhood in the suburbs made an impression on young Cheech. "I remember the orange groves in Granada Hills," he says. "It was really an idyllic (perfect) boy's country life."

"Only English was spoken in our house," he said in a 1992 *Los Angeles Times* interview. "My parents would speak Spanish with my grandparents when they didn't want me to understand." As an adult, however, he made a point to learn Spanish in order to teach it to his own children.

Cheech was an eager baseball player as a boy, so his early role models were baseball players, including most of the Los Angeles Dodgers, such as pitchers

"Only English was spoken in our house. My parents would speak Spanish when they didn't want me to under— stand."

Don Drysdale and Sandy Koufax. His most favorite ballplayer was Willie Mays, despite the fact that he played for the rival team, the San Francisco Giants. "I really loved him. For me, he was the ultimate ballplayer." As far as entertainers or Hollywood figures go, he says, "At the time, there was a dearth (lack) of Latino public figures for me to look up to," and typical of many young boys, baseball was his real obsession.

"My family taught me that education is really important," says Cheech.

"My family taught me that education was really important. In our family, education was first and foremost. My dad had a small amount of college, and academics (studying and homework) were always stressed—of course, I learned it was important to clean your room, too," he jokes.

But learning was always fun for Cheech. "The quest for knowledge became a really exciting factor for me, that and playing sports and the discovery of girls. What else do you need?" Though he says he enjoyed subjects like history and biology, English teachers, such as high school teacher Father Donovan, encouraged Cheech to study writing and literature.

Educated in Catholic schools, Cheech attended De La Salle Elementary School in San Fernando until eighth grade and then Alemany Catholic High School, where he was a straight-A student. It was in college, he says, that his eyes were opened to the world outside of the church.

His most favorite ballplayer was Willie Mays. "I really loved him. For me, he was the ultimate ballplayer."

Chapter 2
Cheech Meets Chong

Cheech left college just 8 credits short of his degree.

After working his way through college as a dishwasher and janitor, he quit school only eight credits short of a bachelor of arts degree in English from California State University at Northridge. He chose to take pottery classes and enjoyed them so much—for a short time—that he thought he had found what he wanted to do for the rest of his life. But with the growing intensity of the Vietnam War during the mid-1960s, this dream was cut short.

Many young men his age, between 18 and 21, were being drafted. That means that the US government would order them to join the armed forces and fight in the war. Many Americans opposed the war, including Cheech. He chose to move to Canada to avoid the draft. "I had had it with school at that point and was off to seek my fame and fortune. I didn't get the degree, but I got the education, and I thought that was most important. I couldn't unlearn what I had learned," he says.

Cheech moved to Vancouver, a large city in the Canadian province of British Columbia. He began driving a truck for a carpet company to earn a living. Soon he met Tommy Chong, whose family owned a nightclub called the Shanghai Junk.

Chong had already begun a comedy group called City Works, which performed improvisational comedy. That means they worked without a script, taking suggestions from the audience and making up funny skits on the spot. He asked Cheech to join and they soon become friends. From that

He moved to Canada to avoid the draft for the Vietnam War.

friendship, the improvisational comedy troupe Cheech and Chong was born.

By 1972, their act, which made fun of people who used drugs, especially marijuana, took off. They began performing in nightclubs. That year they also approached record maker Lou Adler to make their first comedy album, *Cheech and Chong*, which featured the crazy nun Sister Mary Elephant in charge of a room full of energetic high-

Cheech (left) and Chong (right) starred together in Cheech & Chong's Nice Dreams.

school kids. Two years later they had earned four gold albums as well as many top-ten singles, including "Basketball Jones." Their third album, *Los Cochinos* (the Dirty Ones), brought them a Grammy Award.

In 1976, after the release of their album *Sleeping Beauty*, Cheech and Chong stopped making records and started writing scripts for their own movie. Their first effort was *Up In Smoke*, which was released in 1978. The movie's huge success (it cost $2 million to make but earned over $104 million in worldwide box-office ticket sales) established Cheech and Chong as Hollywood darlings.

Chong would direct all six of their next movies, but the movies were a mutual effort with equal input from Cheech. They had become such good friends they could almost read each other's minds. Cheech describes his relationship with Chong like this: "It's like music. You know, when you start a riff and the other guy chimes in. We've

Cheech met Tommy Chong in Vancouver, British Columbia.

known each other so long and have such a backlog of experiences together." Before the duo split up in 1985, they released a total of eight movies, including *Cheech and Chong's Next Movie* in 1980, *Cheech and Chong's Nice Dreams* in 1981, *Things Are Tough All Over* in 1983, and *Cheech and Chong's The Corsican Brothers* in 1984.

By the time he decided to make his own movies, Cheech was ready to drop

Below: From Cheech and Chong's Next Movie.

the act of the marijuana-smoking hippie. Although he made jokes about the uselessness of smoking marijuana in the form of Cheech the character, the real Cheech was not actually the same person he played in his movies. Even reporters who interviewed him at the time seemed surprised at his "intelligence and articulateness."

His partner, Chong, wanted to continue with the same movies, but Cheech was ready to send a new message to Hollywood. He explained his feelings this way in a *Los Angeles Times* interview: "We had grown out of those guys. At some point, it becomes pathetic and not funny." Still, the experience had made him a household name. "I'm real proud of the legacy," he later commented. "It's like having been in the Beatles or the [Rolling] Stones, something that's a part of society and culture. I would never turn my back on that. If it wasn't for that, I wouldn't be here now."

> **By the time he decided to make his own movies, Cheech was ready to drop the act of the dope-smoking hippie.**

Chapter 3
Cheech on His Own

In 1987, Cheech wrote, directed, and starred without Chong in *Born in East L.A.*

In 1987, Cheech released the first movie in which he not only starred but which he also wrote and directed—*Born in East L.A.* Though some movie critics seemed disappointed (many expected Cheech to bring back his character from his Cheech and Chong days), Latinos did not miss the significant message behind the movie. Looking back, *Born in East L.A.* was surprisingly ahead of its time. It began as a takeoff of the Bruce Springsteen hit song "Born in the U.S.A."

The movie tells the story of Chicano Rudy Robles, whom the Immigration and Naturalization Service *(la migra)* picks up by mistake and deports to Mexico. Because Rudy's family is out of town and he has no identification with him (he left his wallet at home), he's stuck in Mexico, trying to figure out a way to get back to Los Angeles. As one reviewer described it, "[Cheech] tries so hard to be zany, convincing and eventually serious about the poverty that leads so many Mexicans to cross the border."

In a moving moment in the

Cheech wrote and directed Born in East L.A. *Cheech was actually born in East L.A.*

movie, Rudy leads hundreds of Mexicans across the border, overwhelming the Border Patrol, to the tune of Neil Diamond's song "Coming to America." Cheech is very proud of this film. "*Born* was extremely important to me. I had broken up with my partner. I was getting divorced at the same time. I didn't have anything on the horizon except house payments. I knew I wanted to do something else, some kind of social commentary."

Although he did star in one more movie, *Shrimp on the Barbie,* in 1990, and he was the voice of Tito, the streetwise Chihuahua in Disney's animated film *Oliver and Company,* he began to turn his attention to television and music. He says he had been trying to break the barrier for Latinos in television for years, but whether it was his character from the Cheech and Chong movies or simple resistance by television executives, he hadn't been successful. He spent two years developing a series for the Latino comedy troupe Culture

Cheech says he had been trying to break the barrier for Latinos into TV for years, but he hadn't been successful.

Clash for Fox Television, but it never got off the ground. "I had this kind of Latino agenda where I was trying to get this Latino presence on television and get myself rich at the same time," he says.

In 1992, he broke through with a role on *Golden Palace*, a spin-off from the *Golden Girls* series about four retired ladies living in Miami, Florida. In the show he played Chuy Castillos, a divorced transplanted Chicano chef with an attitude from Los Angeles. Though the show was canceled, Cheech never gave up. "I said, 'I'm not going to let these guys defeat me. I am going to make an entry into TV somewhere, somehow.' I just had to keep lowering my head and banging it through the door. They didn't make my faith in myself falter, but my faith in the whole industry process—I was definitely disillusioned."

In 1994, Cheech was cast in the TNT movie *Cisco Kid* in the role of Pancho. The film starred Jimmy Smits as Cisco

> **"I'm not going to let these guys defeat me. I am going to make an entry into TV some—where."**

and was directed by Luis Valdez. The story, based on O. Henry's poem "The Caballero's Way," takes place during the Mexican Revolution which ended in the famous battle won by a small Mexican

Cheech (right) with Jimmy Smits in The Cisco Kid.

army on May 5, 1862, against the French. This victory is still celebrated today in Mexico, but even more enthusiastically in the U.S., as *el Cinco de Mayo*.

Cisco is a man in search of his identity. He was born in California, when it was still part of Mexico, but fought in the Civil War as an American. He travels to Mexico on a secret mission from the U.S. government to supply guns to Mexican rebels, and that's where he meets Pancho, a Mexican revolutionary. "Cisco is probably the first Chicano," commented Smits, a New Yorker of Puerto Rican descent. "There is a whole question of identity: 'Where do I belong?'" His role was particularly attractive to Cheech because it's Pancho, the man committed to his country—Mexico—and to the revolution, who helps Cisco find his identity.

About this time, Marin began to feel his artistic focus turning away from movies and toward his old passion, music.

From time to time, Cheech's love of music pulled his focus away from acting.

Chapter 4
A Musical Break

He likes to record songs for children.

Never leaving his first love, music, and being the father of three, Cheech began to work on a CD for children, *My Name Is Cheech the School Bus Driver*, which was also released in Spanish as *Me Llamo Cheech, el Chofer del Autobus de la Esquela*. Lou Adler, who had produced the Cheech and Chong records, approached Cheech about recording the CD. Adler had produced several children's records at the time, but it was his wife who noticed that few records existed for bilingual children. The project appealed to Cheech for two reasons. As a parent, he wanted to create something his kids could relate to. And this way, he could satisfy his own desire to return to music.

The songs are fun to listen to. For elementary-school children, the record tells the story of Cheech, a bus driver who prepares the kids on the bus for a full day of school, beginning with art class and the song, "Red and Blue and Yellow Too."

He also teaches bigger lessons with songs like "Trading Lunches," which not only encourages kids to explore new worlds through food but also to learn about their classmates. Cheech sings: "You could trade a bowl of guacamole for a plate of ravioli or a cup of minestrone for a ham and cheese on rye. Maybe a cup of Chinese noodles for a hunk of apple strudel or maybe something you never ever tried." The lesson is reinforced with the refrain: "Trading lunches, you might eat something from Greece. Trading lunches could bring about world peace."

His songs are both fun and educa– tional.

In addition, he teaches a little English or Spanish—depending on the version of the CD—with the song, "Tell Me How Do You Say," which is *"Dime Como Se Dice."* in Spanish. Songs like this one were really important, he says. "I strongly support bilingual education, and it worries me that as each generation distances itself further from Mexico, we lose the language of our heritage."

His album became a great success, and the Los Angeles School District even used one of his songs to teach kids about how to mix and use colors. In 1996 he released a second album: *My Name is Cheech the School Bus Driver "Coast to Coast."* According to Cheech, "The music speaks directly to kids in an intelligent way—the songs are fun, but educational."

The CDs also gave him a chance to use the Tex-Mex sound in his songs. "Tex-Mex music is complicated and simple at the same time," he explains. "I believe, in the future, these rhythms will be our children's popular music."

A few years later, Marin would be called to experiment in the culinary (cooking) arts. In 1999 he was approached to develop hot sauces. A lover of spicy food, Cheech was interested in the project but he knew that if they were going to have his name on them, the sauces would have to be really good.

Cheech has some hot sauces named after him.

He agreed to work with a Latino-owned company, the Figueroa Brothers, who had a lot of experience making specialty foods. After several taste tests, Marin had developed three flavors— Gnarly Garlic, Smokin' Chipotle, and his favorite Mojo Mango. "It's really good on fish," he says.

Chapter 5
Back to Movies and Television

Director Robert Rodriguez tapped Marin to appear in three of his films.

By 1995, Cheech's movie career took another positive turn. He starred in Robert Rodriguez's movie *Desperado*, a sequel to Rodriguez's first movie, *El Mariachi*. Immediately after that, he appeared in Rodriguez's next movie, *From Dusk Till Dawn*, where he played three characters, most notably a border patrol officer, for which he actually shaved his mustache.

According to Rodriguez, he had been trying to fill the role for *From Dusk Till Dawn* without much success. In the same interview he says, "I had a number of actors read it and it didn't play at all. Then Cheech read it, and I thought, 'Oh my God, this is gonna be gold.'" Also in 1995, Cheech was the voice of Banzai, one of the dastardly hyenas in Disney's *The Lion King*.

He starred in two more movies in 1996. Along with Samuel L. Jackson, Jeff Goldblum, and Damon Wayans, he starred in *The Great White Hype*, in which he played a character modeled after the Latino head of the World Boxing Council. "The character's just a toady (yes-man), basically," he says. He also starred in *Tin Cup* along with Kevin Costner, playing a golf caddie who is also Costner's best buddy.

Marin came back to television in 1995 in the CBS television drama *Nash Bridges* with Don Johnson. *Nash Bridges* is set in San Francisco, and Cheech plays Johnson's long-time friend and partner Joe Dominguez.

"It's a cop show," he says, "but a lot of it takes place off duty. It explores their personal and familial relationships, and

Cheech finally made it in television in 1995 when *Nash Bridges* became a successful show.

it has a lot of humor. Don Johnson is a wonderful guy to work with, and I love filming in San Francisco." The show was renewed again for the fall 2000 season. After years of knocking on the door to the world of television, Marin seems genuinely pleased with this show. Persistence and hard work eventually do pay off.

Cheech stars with Don Johnson in Nash Bridges.

While enjoying the success of his television show, Cheech decided to branch out yet again. In 2000, he was cast in a play called *The Late Henry Moss.* He plays Esteban, the next door neighbor who is questioned by the sons of Henry Moss, who dies mysteriously. This is a new experience for Marin, who had performed on stage as part of the comedy duo Cheech and Chong but never in a play. One reviewer commented about his performance that although he was new to the theater, he seemed "fully at home."

With daughter Carmen in 1996.

Cheech has three children: Carmen (1980)—his daughter from a previous marriage—and Joe, (1986), and Jasmine, (1993), with his wife Patti. From his experiences, Cheech has this advice for young people today: "The thing I think is most important to emphasize is work hard, practice, be diligent, do the work, because that's the only way you'll get ahead. Everybody has different degrees of talent or innate attributes, but the only way you develop them is through hard work and diligence and with your nose to the grindstone."

With son Joe in 1998.

Hollywood, especially for Latinos, has its ups and downs. Cheech hopes to keep working as much as he can, but he also wants to spend more time with his family and do the things he loves to do, like writing and collecting Chicano art. He owns one of the largest collections of Chicano art, over 100 pieces. "I've always been interested in art, since grade school. I educated myself about art from the time I was in fifth or sixth grade," he says.

Once he got older and could afford to buy art, he began collecting. "Not only did I want to encourage these artists, their work was the best, regardless of race, and the art spoke to me more clearly than any other art I'd seen," he explains.

Just as these artists spoke to him, Cheech's work, his talent, and his sincerity will continue to speak to Latinos and to all audiences, on TV, on CDs, and in the movies.

FILMOGRAPHY

- *Cheech and Chong's Up in Smoke* (1978)
- *Cheech and Chong's Next Movie* (1980)
- *Cheech and Chong's Nice Dreams* (1981)
- *Cheech and Chong: Things are Tough All Over* (1982)
- *It Came from Hollywood* (1982)
- *Still Smokin'* (1983)
- *Yellowbeard* (1983)
- *Cheech and Chong's The Corsican Brothers* (1984)
- *After Hours* (1985)
- *Cheech and Chong—Get Out of My Room* (1985)
- *Born in East L.A.* (1987)
- *Rude Awakening* (1989)
- *Troop Beverly Hills* (1989)
- *Mother Goose Rock 'N Rhyme* (1990)
- *Shrimp on the Barbie* (1990)
- *Oliver and Company* (1990)
- *La Pastorela* (1992)
- *Ring of the Musketeers* (1993)
- *Xuxa*
  Celebration
  with Cheech Marin (1993)
- *Charlie's Ghost—The Secret of Coronado* (1994)
- *Cisco Kid* (1994)
- *Goldy III: The Magic of the Golden Bear* (1994)
- *Lion King* (1994)
- *Million to Juan* (1994)
- *Courtyard* (1995)
- *Desperado* (1995)
- *From Dusk Till Dawn* (1996)
- *The Great White Hype* (1996)
- *Tin Cup* (1996)
- *Paulie* (1998)
- *Nuttiest Nutcracker* (1999)
- *Picking up the Pieces* (2000)
- *SpyKids* (2001)

DISCOGRAPHY

- *"Amorcito Corazón"* (1951)
- *Cheech and Chong* (1971)
- *Big Bambu* (1972)
- *Los Cochinos* (1973)
- *Cheech and Chong's Wedding Album* (1974)
- *Up in Smoke* (1978)
- *Cheech and Chong's Greatest Hit* (1981)
- *My Name is Cheech the School Bus Driver* (1994)
- *Me Llamo Cheech el Chofer del Autobus* (1994)
- *My Name is Cheech the School Bus Driver "Coast to Coast "*(1996)

TELEVISION

- *Golden Palace* (1992)
- *Nash Bridges* (1996)
- *Santo Bugito* (1999)

THEATER

- *The Late Henry Moss* (2000)

Chronology

- 1946, born on July 13 in Los Angeles
- 1956, moves to Granada Hills
- 1964, attends California State University at Northridge
- 1968, moves to Canada, where he meets Tommy Chong
- 1972, records first Cheech and Chong album, *Cheech and Chong*
- 1974, earns Grammy Award for Cheech and Chong's third album, *Los Cochinos*
- 1979, first Cheech and Chong movie, *Up in Smoke*, is released.
- 1987, writes, directs and stars in *Born in East L.A.*
- 1994, releases the CD, *My Name is Cheech the School Bus Driver* in English and Spanish.
- 1995, stars in *Desperado*.
- 1996, stars in *From Dusk Till Dawn, The Great White Hype,* and *Tin Cup*.
- 1996, stars in *Nash Bridges* on CBS-TV.
- 2000, cast in the play *The Late Henry Moss*
- 2001, appears in *SpyKids*

Index